HOW THE WEST
THE
WAS
WHITE-WASHED

CURTARUS KIRK

authorHOUSE®

AuthorHouse™
1663 Liberty Drive
Bloomington, IN 47403
www.authorhouse.com
Phone: 833-262-8899

Published by AuthorHouse 10/05/2020

ISBN: 978-1-6655-0140-8 (sc)
ISBN: 978-1-6655-0232-0 (e)

This book is dedicated to my wife, Monique and my children: Anela, Brendan, and Kyndall. Thank you for allowing me the time to research and develop this historical work.

To Lincoln Sigwald, my college professor that inspired me to see the theory and themes of History and not just the name, dates, and places.

To Holly Miranda, my friend and co-teacher. Your life taught me how to teach with a smile and your death took me to never take life for granted. You will forever live in my memories and I am grateful for knowing you. RIP

Contents

Literature Review ix

Chapter 1   Advancing the Topic 1

Chapter 2   Black Cowboys on the Western Frontier 5

Chapter 3   The White Wash/White Savior Effect 9

Chapter 4   The Hidden Frontier 15

Chapter 5   Bass Reeves (The Real Lone Ranger) 21

Chapter 6   Britt Johnson (The Real Duke) 25

Chapter 7   Nat Love (Deadwood Dick) 29

Chapter 8   Willie Bill Pickett (The Dusky Demon) 33

Chapter 9   Lesser Known Names 37

Chapter 10 The Power of Knowledge 45

Book Reviews 49

Bibliography 51

Literature Review

The American West is often seen from the historical accounts recorded from the beginning of the Civil War to after the Reconstruction Era. Many of the accounts include historians that promote a European/Anglo-Saxon perspective; these accounts have often led readers to stereotypical perspectives concerning minorities. These accounts also give birth to the "white savior" concept in which white men assume the role as savior to lesser races in movies, such as saving the African Americans during slavery or in the case of many White Westerners: being the hero to Native American people. Hollywood's portrayal of Westerners did not happen by accident, but many historians in the late 19th and early 20th centuries purposely ignored the accounts and contributions of other races.

The narrative trope of the white savior is one way the mass communications medium of cinema represents the sociology of race and ethnic relations, by presenting abstract concepts such as morality as characteristics innate, racially and culturally, to white people, not to be found in non-white people. In other words, had Hollywood sought accurate information and represented it in the narratives for shows like *The Lone Ranger*, the show would have been cast with an African American actor since the role was based solely on the life of black lawman, Bass Reeves. A White Savior film is often based on some supposedly true story. Second, it features a nonwhite group or person who experiences conflict and struggle with others that is particularly dangerous or threatening to their life and livelihood.

One of the most noted historians concerning the Western Frontier, Frederick Jackson Turner, quoted in his "Social Forces in American History:" each age finds it necessary to reconsider at least some portion of the past, from points of view furnished by new conditions which reveal the influence and significance of forces not adequately known by the historians of the previous generation. Turner and other historians of the Progressive Era, such as Arthur M. Schlesinger Sr. and Charles Beard, really did not consider a place for race or gender in their perspectives on the Western Frontier. These historians only used the events of the Civil War and Reconstruction because of their impact on white society and various white institutions. The African American existence was only needed as a backdrop to the bravery of white men as they conquered and developed the Western Frontier. Schlesinger Sr. felt that the narrative of African Americans served little purpose in writings except for the fact that the 14th Amendment added citizenship to them and allowed them the opportunity to work the lands given by whites. Schelsinger Sr. ignored black history in his writings but served on the Council of the Association for the Study of Negro Life and History.

Not only did leading historians such as Turner, Schlesigner Sr. and Beard ignore the contributions of African Americans on the Frontier; their ignoring of these facts led to a major gap in the understanding of the true Frontier. The Frontier through their eyes became the standard for how others would view history. Sadly to say, the impact of other races was reduced to a small part of a complex puzzle. Their writings reduced the importance of other races by simply not finding them worth mentioning much outside of the races' support to the white male cause. If nothing else, these historians aided in establishing the concepts of "white savior" and "whitewashing" in historical representations.

The quasi-historical novels of James Fennimore Cooper, Walter Edmonds, and Conrad Richter follow Turner, Schlesigner Sr. and Beard in an attempt to show the Western Frontier as the Manifesto of the United States. In their writings, the main focus is on the white settlers that braved the threats from Indians and the Mexicans to solidify the dream of Western Expansion. Cooper is well-known for popularizing historical fiction that has been the foundation for Western movies. His writings support the theory of "whitewashed history" and contribute to fictitious, imaginary viewpoints of the West. Along with the other writers mentioned previously, Cooper's viewpoint promotes white dominance on the American Frontier and stereotypes other races.

Why are the contributions of African Americans important to the West? The founding of the Colonial National Monument (CNM) in 1931 is a case study on ways African Americans were intentionally written out of American history until well into the twentieth century. According to modern historian, Matthew Wills, African Americans were left out of important historical moments like the American West for the purpose of control. This control, in their opinion, would keep one race supreme and the other race inferior, as well as suffocate any controversy that would arise in later narratives. Dr. Roger Hardaway, another modern-day historian, supports Wills' claims of leaving African American history out of Hollywood and textbooks. Hardaway believes that it was historians like Turner who gave blacks a helpless look on the frontier in his article, "Segregation on the Frontier." He suggests that if it was known that African Americans were able to sustain their own way of life on the Frontier, the dependency of needing white leadership would not exist in Hollywood. To support his thesis, he points at black settlements in the West. Perhaps the most famous all-black frontier settlement was Nicodemus, Kansas. Black promoters of an all-black settlement chose a spot on the western Kansas prairie to establish Nicodemus. They filed homestead claims and mapped out town lots on part of their land. They then went back East to make speeches and distribute brochures encouraging people to move to the proposed town.

According to Hardaway Kenneth Wiggins Porter, a University of Oregon history professor, there were closer to eight thousand, maybe nine thousand black cowboys. That would be about 25 percent of the 35,000 cowboys in the frontier cattle industry. Porter suggests that white historians such as Turner and Beard were writing their narratives for white audiences. However, since there were few blacks that could write their stories or memoirs, popular culture took the white narratives as the truth and ignored other stories. He also suggests that Hollywood had to be biased in their portrayals of heroes due to the segregation and racial tension in the United States. Even though more attempts to include stories of African-American cowboys were made after World War II, Porter believes the foundation of what a cowboy should look like was already set. In summation, there were a lot of African Americans on the frontier, and many were cowboys. For a variety of reasons, they have not been noted in our histories or popular literature. African-American cowboys may still be underrepresented in popular accounts of the West, but the work of scholars such as Katz and Hardaway and cowboys like Hearn keep the memories and undeniable contributions of the early African-American cowboys alive.

Chapter

1

Advancing the Topic

My research in this field will further investigate the scope of omissions on African Americans from history. It will encourage historians to take a look at how leaving important pieces out of history have led to the stereotypes of many races and the dominance of others. The research will also cause Hollywood to evaluate its historical inaccuracies and perspectives on African Americans' roles in movies. Deeper research into this discovery will allow other lesser-known African Americans heroes to emerge throughout history, in this field and in others. As these stories are uncovered, a new sense of black pride will surface and have an impact on the present-day identity of African Americans.

It is with clear understanding that black cowboys have not been invited into most classrooms or institutions of historical learning. In fact, even a Google search only produces a small amount of information on the topic. After conducting a deep inquiry of black cowboys from educators and historians, I concluded that only a small amount of information is known on the topic. Cowboys like Wyatt Earp, Doc Holliday, and Jesse James are well-known heroes of the Western Frontier legacy even though their stories have been fictionalized for the sake of Hollywood. In actuality, presenting cowboys like Bass Reeves, Britton Johnson, Willie M. «Bill» Pickett, and Nate Love, also known as Deadwood Dick would add another perspective on the diversity of the West and its heroes. In presenting new information on this topic, the doorway to a diverse West is inevitable. Mexican, Native American, and Asian history will expand so that others can see that the West Frontier needs to be studied and placed in the history books correctly.

This research can extend the field beyond just changing the narratives of the American West and history, but the social conscience of a people that are still being impacted by false or incomplete teachings in schools. When the revelations of false perspectives and hidden facts are made known to this generation, we can begin to make strides in correcting a lot of fact history being taught in school. Students will begin to appreciate that American history is not solely one-sided and recognize that the other sides make one complete thought. Understanding that history is the foundation of learning is key to changing the narratives of today as well. For so long, Americans have seen white heroes from the West grace the screen. This not only promoted whites as the master race, but implied that other races were not as important. My research will show that every race was important to the foundation of the West and that other heroes (the forgotten ones) were significant in the Frontier.

Lastly, my research will show the other side of the story. The story that was left out by Frederick Jackson Turner and other historians. The impact Turner's *The Significance of the Frontier* made on history changed the way historians viewed the West. My research will advance the understanding of black cowboys in the West. This extension gives new insight into a little known topic and brings a new element to the West. The topic, I must admit, has a controversial undertone which will no doubt cause us to review our stance of racism in history telling. This controversy is not worth shying from the topic but welcome as it will push the field to explore methods of bringing black cowboys to the forefront.

Methods and Theoretical Frameworks

This book will fill in some of the gaps left by historians that sought to present the American West as a victory for European men only. It will not only highlight important characters, contributions, and events, but it will show the importance of a culture that lacks heroes from this important period. This book will also provide an accurate account of history where African American cowboys played an important role in the establishment of the West. It will combat some of the fictional cowboy portrayals by African Americans that exist more for entertainment than empowerment. Lastly, this book will close the gap of white dominance that continues to dominate both Hollywood and history books.

My first method in exposing the true West is to show why the need for "whitewashing" history is essential in maintaining white dominance in the United States. This book proves the theory that leaving black cowboys out of Hollywood and history was done to create an image of the "white savior." It is no accident that Hollywood has aided historians like Turner in presenting the West, a West that is absent of major contributions from other races. Hollywood is responsible for so much of the brainwashing in the American culture; Americans have been taught what to think, what to like and dislike, and what is "real." For the most part, Hollywood has depicted cowboys as white men of bravery such as the case with Wyatt Earp. For the viewers, this image of "white savior" has caused the white race to be the most trusted race in modern-day America. This was no accident, but if we look into Westerns, the hero for the weak has always been that of the white male race.

Many historians can agree that the brainwashing of slaves was similar in that slaves were made to feel that their master was their savior when in fact he was their oppressor. Hollywood created the white male as the savior in the West and thereby placed the white cowboy as the most important part of the Western Frontier. It is important to note that legendary Western movie star, John Wayne, was loved by multiple races for his heroic persona. However, John Wayne was also racist in many regards. In the interview with Playboy magazine from 1971, the actor born Marion Morrison states among other things, "I believe in white supremacy." Regardless of his candidacy, Wayne's statement will continue to be overlooked due to his popularity in Western movies. Many of the films that Wayne played in rest on a completely racist ideal, which damages and stigmatizes non-white cultures, and claims America for white people.

My next method in exposing the true West is to show the importance of other races. This supports the theory that white cowboys were not as dominant as made out to be in television shows and movies. By showing what other races contributed to the real cowboys' narrative, these added perspectives contradict what many historians have taught as the American West. The exposed history disapproves the notion that the American West was a victory for whites and instead shares the victory with other races. If the American culture understood that many of the fashions worn by cowboys were from the Mexican culture or that African Americans sang most of the songs on the ranch (that became the building block for country music), the stigma that the West was "white" would have to be corrected.

My final method is to show that real black cowboys had their stories or portions of their stories stolen and given to white actors to portray. Most of the African American cowboys were unable to read or write, so few records of their lives exist. In order to right this wrong, a true account must be given to the black cowboys that lived these stories and African American actors must be casted to play them. These stories would have added value to the African American cultures had both Hollywood and historians given them the credit they deserved. By telling the real stories and not those with the intent to bring comedy or promote the grandiosity of a white counterpart, African Americans can see that their culture did not just go from slavery straight to the Jim Crow Laws, but had an impact on the Western Frontier.

Chapter

2

Black Cowboys on the Western Frontier

Unique to the United States, the Old West wields a powerful influence on the American imagination that can still be seen in numerous aspects of the nation's culture, such as clothing lines and movies. Unfortunately, as is the case with most other periods, historic acknowledgements of minorities' (Mexican and African Americans) contributions to the West are still not complete. Only recently, within the last few decades, have American scholars and the film industry earnestly begun to correct this period. The fact remains, however, that with little advancement from Hollywood or historians, the contributions of African American cowboys are rarely discussed or analyzed for accuracy. Instead fictitious characters such as Jamie Foxx as Django, Cleavon Little as the sheriff in Blazing Saddles, and Denzel Washington's gun-slinging character in the Magnificent Seven are used to show an attempt to quiet racial tensions, but not to uncover the "whitewashing of the American West." In fact, I dare say that these attempts have given more recognition to their white counterparts than the actual African American lead characters. It can also be noted that these attempts have been wasted due to the lack of historical accuracy in the movies. These historical inaccuracies portray the concept of black cowboys as fictional whereas Kurt Russell and Val Kilmer's portrayal of Wyatt Earp and Doc Holliday is more believable since there is historical accuracy.

Even with Hollywood's best attempts, the American West portrayal on the silver screen has never conveyed the reality that has been left out of the history books and textbooks. The most common image of the cowboy is a gun-toting, boot-wearing, white man like John Wayne or Clint Eastwood. But it's safe to say the Hollywood portrayal of the Wild West is a whitewashed version of the reality. As a child, this depiction caused me to look to white men as heroes because this was all that Hollywood presented. This was the portrayal of "hero" for all African American children. It also created a mentality that I, as an African American, would accept for many years---my own inferiority.

Not only can Hollywood be blamed for "white-washing" history, but many historians skewed our perceptions in an attempt to paint the United States government as a supreme power or better stated ambitious, as presented by Frederick Jackson Turner's *The Significance of the Frontier in American History.* This whitewashed portrayal of cowboys by Hollywood shows not only a failure to research, but it creates a culture where one race becomes more important than another. As a child, I remember receiving Cowboys and Indians action figures. The cowboys were always white men and schoolchildren were taught that Native Americans were savages, so it was only natural to have the cowboy toys defeat the Indian toys. This along with the Westerns my grandfather watched religiously on Saturdays created an inferiority complex that was unknown to me at the time. The notion that whites were better controlled my mind and actors like John Wayne, Clint Eastwood, and other white Western actors became my heroes.

In this book, we will examine both Hollywood and how many Western historians intentionally created a master race by building the American West from the perspective of white male heroes. These men are seen as the gun-slingers, lawmen, and brave heroes in an attempt to "whitewash history." This book will also show the modern struggles

African Americans are facing in Hollywood today when it comes to being the heroes in movies due to the white dominance that was created by false teachings and portrayals. In discrediting Hollywood, the truth of Westerns has to be revealed, such as characters being created based on real African American cowboys, but having white actors portraying them. The reality that other races such as African Americans, Mexicans, and Asians submitting to the heroic white lead characters has to be exposed as racial superiority so that the "white savior" generalization leaves Hollywood Westerns. Finally, in order to delete the "whitewashing" of history, Hollywood must examine the way black cowboys are being presented on the big screen. Although there has been attempts over the years, Hollywood cannot continue to place African American actors in fictitious roles in order to boost movie revenues, but with the intent of correcting itself.

The Negro Cowboys by Philip Durham and *Los Vaqueros: Our First Cowboys* by Sammy Munson are two examples of literature that support the theory that not all cowboys were white men. Even though one book is about African American cowboys and the other one about Mexican cowboys, both books show that the narrative of "whitewashed" cowboys is fictional. In fact, it can be fairly stated that many of the contributions attributed to white cowboys is not true. When African American cowboys entered the Great Plains after the Civil War to work on the long overland drives that linked Texas to the Kansas railheads, they were merely continuing a centuries-old pattern rooted in the American South, Mexico, the Caribbean, southern Iberia, and perhaps even West Africa. In fact, Terry Jordan, a geographer who has thoroughly studied the diffusion and material culture of cattle ranching, notes that African slaves were the vaqueros for the herds in southwestern Spain by the sixteenth century. This African labor-based Iberian model was transferred first to the Caribbean, and from there to Mexico and the North American Atlantic coast, where it eventually combined with Germanic- and Celtic-derived cattle herding traditions. They, their predecessors, and their successors rode on the long cattle drives, joined the cavalry, set up small businesses, and fought on both sides of the law. Some of them became famous: Jim Beckwourth, the mountain man; Bill

Pickett, king of the rodeo; Cherokee Bill, the most dangerous man in Indian Territory; and Nat Love, who styled himself "Deadwood Dick."

It is interesting to note that as a history teacher in the public school system, my content nor do standards cover any of the names mentioned above. In fact, when I taught fifth grade, the standards covered the Reconstruction Period through the present day, which means that the Western Frontier was covered. Only names like Jesse James, Sitting Bull, George Custer, and Wyatt Earp were mentioned and like my students, I thought this was the foundation of the great Western Frontier. I had no idea that the foundation of the West was deeper than these names. I had no idea that men of my own race contributed so much to the establishment of the West. In many of the ways that the slaves built the American South, the black ranchers, cowboys, and lawmen built the West.

The inaccuracies of history tend to lay the framework for the ignorance of a culture. Removing or changing the narrative changes the perception of a culture, and many students in classrooms across the United States are taught to value one race's heroes without learning the value of their own. Could this misconstrued narrative be why the white race is the most trusted in business, education, and even religion? What would happen if the truth surrounding the American Frontier was taught from various narratives instead of the most common one presented?

Chapter

3

The White Wash/
White Savior Effect

With so many heroes on both sides of the color spectrum, it leads us to wonder why these heroes are not as well-known as Jesse James, Doc Holliday, and Billy the Kid. Historians would lead us to believe that the timing of important facts had to be left out due to the sensitivity of race during the periods of segregation especially in the South. However, Hollywood twice portrayed the *Lone Ranger* as a white actor. The first portrayal could be justified by timing as the United States was dealing with racial tension, but the second portrayal was unjustifiable. Take into account that the film was released in 2013 while the President of the United States at the time was a man of color. Not only was the main character whose life was based on black lawman Bass Reeves played by a white actor (Armie Hammer), but for the first ever the role of the Indian, Tonto, was given to a white actor (Johnny Depp). It can be debated that when the original *Lone Ranger* was created in 1949, information was difficult to come by. There were no internet sources to connect us to true knowledge, and the main writers of history were of white race.

As pointed out above, Frederick Jackson Turner duly notes that with every generation, more information will be discovered. However, this added information was not taken into consideration in 2013 where information was made readily available through technology. Having white actors play other races, often in ways that mock, is as old as the film industry itself. African-Americans have long felt the full brunt of the 'whitewashing' of roles as have other races. What is amazing, however, is that the controversy surrounding the remake of the *Lone Ranger* had nothing to do with a white actor playing the role that should have absolutely been given to an African American actor; the major fallout was the casting of Johnny Depp in the role of the Indian, Tonto.

Hollywood issued many statements regarding the casting of Johnny Deep as Tonto, but issued no statements on Armie Hammer playing the main character after it was proven that the character was based on a black lawman. When asked about white actors playing roles designed for minorities, the Hollywood elite suggested that white actors do better at the box office than minority actors. Hollywood also argues that when it comes to overseas marketing value, white actors do better than minority actors in starring roles. "The myth that 'black doesn't travel' would be laughable if its perpetuation weren't so damaging. From Will Smith to Denzel Washington to David Oyelowo, the work of black actors is consumed and celebrated in markets across the globe," says David White, National Executive Director of the actors' union SAG-AFTRA. The recent breakout of movies like *The Black Panther* and *Get Out* support the claim that black actors are now being accepted as cross-over actors. So, if it's not the money, because note the *Lone Ranger* remake was a box office disaster, then what could it be? Maybe Hollywood, like Frederick Jackson Turner, is not ready to celebrate African Americans as heroes on the Frontier besides being a fictional character or great sidekick. Bill Picket was a "famous" Black cowboy who toured the U.S., Canada, Mexico, South America, and England, and he was inducted into the National Rodeo Hall of Fame 40 years after his death. Had he not been banned from competing against White cowboys, he might have become one of the greatest record-setters in the field. Why does this matter? The cowboy is one of the most enduring and iconic cultural images of America, and Black people along with other people of color have been erased from this narrative.

Before we go any further, we have to address the critics that would say that African Americans have been seen in many Westerns, especially in leading roles after World War 2. As stated above, historian Matthew Hughey suggests: in order to continue white dominance in films, a black actor would need the support of a "good" white person to aid the black actor in their cause. If we were looking at this theory as movie critics, we would see Hughey's thesis is accurate. In the movies, *Django Unchained, Blazing Saddles, Posse,* and the remake of *The Magnificent Seven,* all of the main black actors were only successful because of the "white savior" cast alongside them. Even though *Django Unchained* pushed the lines of racial overtones like no other movie presently, the mere fact remains that the racism toward blacks was overshadowed by the love and compassion of the white character, Dr. King Schultz. It would be Dr. Schultz who rescued a poor, helpless slave named Django from the chains of his captors. It was Dr. Schultz who clothed, fed, and eventually trained Django how to shoot a gun. Throughout the movie, the compassion Dr. Schultz had for the black lead was displayed thoroughly, even to the point of risking his own life for the black mistreatment of slaves. The portrayal of Dr. Schultz was so powerful that the actor that played him won an Academy Award while the main character played by African American actor, Jamie Foxx, wasn't even a nominee. This type of Hollywood persuasion is nothing new. Throughout the history of film-making, black actors, even in leading roles, have had to depend on "white saviors" in movies. So you may question some of these explanations, because Dr. Schultz did die and so did the white characters in *The Magnificent Seven.* However, a closer look at these movies shows us an interesting fact, white savior actors always die saving the black leading character. This would conclude that in order for a black leading character to be successful, he needs a "white savior" aiding him on his mission. This type of leading by Hollywood paints whites in a hero light even if the apparent villain is white. So, what happens is the "white savior" role is overly loving so that the white villain is overshadowed and the black and white audience loves the "white savior" more than the white villain or the black hero.

The practice of "whitewashing" film is commonplace in Westerns, as the need for racist stereotypes of minorities is important to the ranking of cultures in American history. Native Americans need to serve as an opponent to Western Expansion, the Asians serve as mere pawns to the advancement of railroad lines, and African Americans who are grateful to be free serve as porters and butlers. Is there any wonder that in today's modern world whites are seen as superior to other races? Rewind back to Frederick Jackson Turner for one brief moment and the "whitewashing" of history will make perfect sense. The key to changing history is simply not to mention all of the major players as Turner made sure to omit everyone but the white males from his historical accounts. By leaving out information, Hollywood was successful in altering stories from black cowboys and giving those stories to white actors.

In his 1907 autobiography, cowboy Nat Love recounts his stories of life on the frontier. In his story, Love describes the scene of Dodge City, Kansas and his life of moving massive herds of cattle, drinking with Billy the Kid, and participating in shootouts with Native Americans. According to Love, "A braver, truer set of men never lived than these wild sons of the plains whose home was in the saddle and their couch, mother earth, with the sky for a covering," he wrote. "They were always ready to share their blanket and their last ration with a less fortunate fellow companion and always assisted each other in the many trying situations that were continually coming up in a cowboy's life." Surreally, his story was not turned into a motion picture by Hollywood producers; instead parts of his life story went to making movies for white actors, John Wayne and Clint Eastwood. The 1956 Western movie, *The Searchers,* starred John Wayne; however, the movie was based on the life of Britt Johnson, an ex-slave and Frontier hero. In 1971, John Wayne told *Playboy* he believed in white supremacy until blacks were educated to the point of responsibility. No wonder John Wayne was seen as the greatest Western movie star and seen as an American hero. Wayne embodied bravery, compassion, and a heroic persona. It is too bad the stories he represented were often fictitious or based on the life of someone else. Jim Beckwourth's story would also be taken in order to make another white actor famous in the 1951 movie, *Tomahawk*.

In addition to whitewashing television in Hollywood, music was also infiltrated by Whites who took credit for the work and talents of minorities. Musicians during the segregation period like Little Richard, Chuck Berry, and Otis Redding have all stated that their music was stolen, not borrowed by white musicians for the sake of taking their craft to white audiences. Eventually white musicians like Pat Boone, the Rolling Stones, and the Beach Boys would make more money than the black artists they stole the music from, and many of their versions are more memorable than the black artists' such as Satisfaction sung by the Rolling Stones, but written by Otis Redding.

It can be suggested that in order to make a more dominant white America, the stories of black cowboys were stolen to promote stronger white hero cowboys. With no real black historians to fight for black cowboys during those times, it was easy for the stories to be stolen and given to white producers. Sadly, just like songs that have been popularized by white singers, movies, too, have become more popular while portrayed by white actors.

The 1996 Western comedy, *The Cherokee Kid,* paid homage to the memory of Nat Love. The character was more fictitious than accurate, and any sense of historical accuracy was lost in the puns and jokes displayed in the movie. Dare we say that this was an attempt by Hollywood to give black audiences a watered down version of the American West as to please blacks by their inclusion, but to essentially diminish and hide the historical accuracy of Nat Love's true contributions. The mere fact that the lead role went to Sinbad, a comedian, shows the intent of Hollywood to turn what could have been a great historical film into a comedy. Not only was Sinbad given the lead role, but his portrayal of the character was based around being considered a clown more than a cowboy for the majority of the movie. The Nat Turner character was based on a namesake more than historical facts. At best the movie showed diversity in the West, but due to its comedic tone, the movie did not highlight or advance the topic of black cowboys.

Here lies the case with so many Westerns produced after World War 2. Black Westerns were either "whitewashed, given a "white savior," or fictional. One of the few representations of black cowboys in mainstream entertainment is the fictional Josh Deets in Texas novelist Larry McMurtry's *Lonesome Dove* where an ex-slave turned cowboy serves as a scout on a Texas-to-Montana cattle drive. Deets was inspired by real-life Bose Ikard, an African-American cowboy who worked on the Charles Goodnight and Oliver Loving cattle drive in the late-19th century. In reality, the truth behind the making of *Lonesome Dove* supports the thesis statement above, as Lonesome Dove was originally set to star white actors, John Wayne and Robert Duvall, before finally setting on the movie cast. It should also be mentioned that *Lonesome Dove's* intent was not to tell the story of Bose Ikard, but to tell a great Western story. This proves once again that Hollywood's intent is not for historical accuracy, but to entertain.

A three-legged dog walks into the saloon and announces, "I'm a looking for the man who shot my paw." (Old Western Joke)

Chapter

4

The Hidden Frontier

In order for Hollywood to do justice for African Americans in Westerns, Hollywood must first search out the truth of the West. The very culture of the cowboys refers to a style of ranching introduced by Spanish colonists in the early 16th century. During this time most of the ranch owners were Spanish and ranch workers were Native Americans. The first white cowboys did not arrive in the West until centuries later and even though historians do not have accurate numbers, it has been suggested that by the 19th century one in three cowboys were Mexican and one in four cowboys were African Americans. This shows us that the West was more diverse than Westerns movies portray, especially when Native Americans and Asians have to be factored into the equation. The style of most Hollywood Westerns such as the hats, bandanas, spurs, and lassos are all contributions of Mexican heritage that have obviously been plagiarised as White contributions. This is why today when a minority wears cowboy boots or a cowboy hat, he/she is considered to be acting "white" and why Country music is seen as "white people music."

Hollywood chose not to show that most of the songs sung on the ranch were created by African American cowboys.

In popular Western television shows like *Bonanza* and *Big Valley,* you see prominent white families that are successful ranchers; however, to be historically accurate, these families would not be doing the hard labor required of ranchers. Most of the ranching work was left up to black slaves and after the Civil War, blacks stayed on as ranchers or cowhands. Neither show endorsed the reality that blacks served as ranchers and instead presents the false reality that most of the work was done by whites. In the long run, this thinking serves as an argument in today's politics as it can be viewed by many rich whites that success comes through getting your hands dirty, when in fact success has always hung on the contributions of others in the background. Was Hollywood afraid that including other races for historical accuracy would be a blow to white dominance? Blacks rarely appear in Western fiction, as noted by several historians. Western fiction, historians contend, started in 1902 with Owen Wister's' *The Virginian.* There are romanticized cattlemen in the novel but no African Americans. Wister visited the west, but he went fishing and hunting with cattlemen or guides. "He saw cowboys at leisure, but rarely at work." Historians think that Wister shared the racial prejudice of his times. Wister's work, historians feel, shows an admiration for the Anglo–Saxon, the conquering white man.

It would seem fitting to say that Wister, Turner, and Hollywood failed to mention just how diverse the Western Frontier was. In order to see both sides of the argument, let's entertain the notion that due to segregation being lawfully enforced during their times, it was not smart to include other races in the cinema. Even with such an argument, this still does not constitute a removal of the truth. To say that a racially prejudiced time would hinder writers and historians from telling the truth is a good reason for today's Hollywood to change or challenge the status quo. Since we are not living in a world where we are afraid to present new findings, it is important for Hollywood to show what Wister and Turner left out, rather than building on their mishaps or lack of information.

Attracted by high wages and freedom, the cowboys included former slaves, Mexicans, Civil War soldiers, and Native Americans. Even though there were racial tensions, many of these groups found harmony on the ranch. There was also many cases of interracial marriage and children in the American West that would show a different perspective than Hollywood portrayed. These small nuggets of truth show that in order for white dominance to be shown in Westerns, historical truths had to be ignored. Even if Hollywood's goal was not to show white dominance, it has to be responsible for the historical accounts it left out that led to white dominance.

As stated previously, with the advancement in knowledge and technology, why hasn't Hollywood sped up its approach on Western movies today that start black actors? Many would suggest that the latest roles that star black actors is an attempt to right some of the wrongs; however, until black actors are allowed to play real black heroes, history will continue to be in error. Black lawmen like Bass Reeves will continue to be played out by white actors attempting to gain success by portraying the *Lone Ranger* or through characters like Marshall Matt Dillon on the show *Gunsmoke*. Until Hollywood stops "whitewashing" history, we will continue to see blacks either playing fictional characters with strong white counterparts or Westerns turned into comedies.

The major question is: Is Hollywood ready for the truth? Could Hollywood show the truth of black cowboys without the entertainment portion that takes away from the historical accuracy of truth? I suggest that it can be both knowledgeable and beneficial for Hollywood to create a historically correct version of black cowboys. The Black Panther, as stated earlier, was a prime example that African Americans support black films done on a universal stage. With the boom of social media, African Americans have taken a more direct approach to advocate for the inclusion of black lives in popular media and for the acknowledgement of their lives and culture in general. With the support of Black Power advocates, Hollywood will only reach more success by producing a movie with black actors playing real black heroes.

If the "whitewashing" of history continues, the true cultural advancements in African American Studies will continue to diminish. Not only will the West be seen as a victory for white males, but the contributions of African Americans will be highly debated. The fact that some historians are suggesting that the role of black cowboys is small at best and less significant than the book describes is an early sign of things to come. Not only will the history of black cowboys be debated, but the white cowboy domination will continue to be the platform when it comes to the Western Frontier. Even though Frederick Jackson Turner's book has been debated by modern historians on certain content, the one content that hasn't been debated until now is his removal of other races from the Western Frontier.

The real account of the West has to mention the contributions of the black cowboys. It was these cowboys that traveled miles throughout the West driving cattle while many of their counterparts were away at war. It has to be mentioned that black cowboys served as lawmen, and many protected newly formed black towns from Indian raids and prejudiced white men. The Buffalo Soldiers (a black regime) were given the sole purpose of protecting white settlers from raids as they moved forward with Western expansion.

Matthew Hughes, whom we alluded to earlier in the book, stated that the "white savior" image has to be erased in order for true history to be taught. Historians must present another version of Turner's accounts on the Frontier to establish a new sense of truth. Even if this means the United States will lose some of its favorable viewings, the reality of the Frontier must be explained through diverse viewpoints and cultural lenses. White men and their ambition can no longer be the center point for the Frontier, but the advancements of the West must be explored and documented correctly so that all races are represented properly. This means that my work serves as a launching pad to revisit what has been taught and explore new fields of study on this particular topic. Next, Hollywood must give an account for the inaccurate portrayals of black cowboys and seek to build more Western movies that establish the importance of black cowboys in the West.

Maybe when these actions are considered and submitted, African American history will add more heroes from the Western Frontier to establish a complete history. These actions will also go a long way in teaching African Americans the pride of knowing that black cowboys were more than comedic overtones for movies or in need of white counterparts overshadowing them in Westerns. "Whitewashing" history does nothing for the culture being deprived of the truth. Considering that the truth has been presented in history, it is pretty safe to conclude that more research and understanding needs to be given to this topic.

> *"Never approach a bull from the front, a horse from the rear or a fool from any direction."*

> **(Old West Proverb)**

Chapter

5

Bass Reeves
(The Real Lone Ranger)

*Portrait of U.S. Marshal Bass Reeves | Courtesy of
the National Park Service at Fort Smith*

Bass Reeves is one of the greatest American Frontier lawmen not mentioned in modern history books. His life inspired many of the legends that have been contributed to Wyatt Earp in the movie, *Tombstone*, and the famous television show, *The Lone Ranger*. To be honest, the revelation of Bass Reeves was revealed to me by accident. Through Social Media someone posted what I assumed was a false claim concerning the story idea of the show, *The Lone Ranger*. The post referred to Bass Reeves, an African American lawman, and how his story was used as the backdrop for the concept of the show. Immediately, I sought out to dispute this claim, however, unbenounced to me, the post was actually accurate.

Bass Reeves was born into slavery in 1838, in Crawford County,

Arkansas. He was owned by plantation owner, William Reeves, a farmer and Arkansas state legislator. His first name was from his grandfather, Basse Washington. As a young boy, Bass served as a water boy, which means he was in charge of keeping the slaves in the field hydrated. When he came to age, Bass served in the fields with his parents. According to records, William Reeves moved his operations and slaves to Grayson County, Texas.

When the Civil War broke out, Texas sided with the Confederacy and George Reeves, the son of William Reeves, took Bass with him to fight. It was during the Civil War that Bass and Reeves parted ways. There have been speculations concerning this parting of ways, and no one is really sure of the reasoning. However, the popular account is that Bass heard that if the North was victorious then the slaves would be free. Instead of waiting for the conclusion of the war, Bass simply ran off and fled to the Indian Territory where he took refuge with Seminole, Cherokee, and Creek Indians. As the war concluded, Reeves settled down in Van Buren, Arkansas, and worked as a farmer.

In 1875 Judge Isaac C. Parker took over the Fort Smith federal court and one of his first assignments was to commission Reeves as a deputy U.S. Marshal, making Reeves one of the first African Americans to receive this commission. Reeves worked for thirty-two years as a deputy marshal in Indian Territory. He quickly became a celebrity throughout the West, standing at more than six feet and weighing 180 pounds. Known for his skilled rifle and quick draw, Reeves was most known for his wit, as he outsmarted many of his criminals by wearing costumes.

Art Burton's biography, *Black Gun, Silver Star: The Life and Legend of Frontier Marshal Bass Reeves*, tells the story of how Reeves used his wit to outsmart criminals. One day Reeves was running down a pair of Texan murderers when they got the drop on him. Reeves encountered the two men on the road, and they asked him if he was Bass Reeves. Reeves said that he was not, and the outlaws pulled their guns on him believing he was indeed the marshal. The outlaws forced him to ride with them until they encountered someone who knew him.

After continuing along for some time, the Texans got tired of holding Reeves hostage, and they ordered him off of his horse so that they could kill him. Like something out of a Western movie, they asked Reeves if he had any last words, to which he replied that he had a letter from his wife that he wanted the killers to read to him. Reeves handed them the letter with shaking hands. As the men took their eyes off Reeves, the marshal drew his gun on the outlaw holding the letter, and the other killer dropped his gun in surprise. Reeves brought them both in. A cunning trickster, Reeves is said to have made use of this same letter a number of times throughout the years.

Bass Reeves married Nellie Jennie, and the pair had ten children: five boys and five girls. Even though Reeves was a lawman, misfortune fell amongst his family. One of his sons, Beenie Reeves, found his wayward wife, Cassie, with another man in bed. As a result, he beat the man unconscious, and then shot his wife to death. Marshal Leo Bennett, Bass's boss, only gave Bass permission to bring his son in after other marshals turned down the job out of fear of what Bass would do. After two weeks, Bass tracked and captured his son in the Oklahoma hills. Bennie was convicted of murder and sentenced to life in prison in Leavenworth Federal Prison in Kansas. Bass stood beside his son through the trial and it is said that he visited his son often in jail. After nearly 12 years, Bennie's sentence was commuted and he returned to Muskogee.

Bass Reeves was credited with over 3,000 arrests in his career and even though he was illiterate, he never brought in the wrong person. Unlike the great Matt Dillion in Gunsmoke, Reeves was never shot in a gun battle. The great lawman was removed from his position in 1907 when Oklahoma gained its statehood. Due to being an African American, Reeves was unable to continue in his position due to Jim Crow laws (state laws at the time) that prohibited blacks from serving in law enforcement. Reeves would only live three years after his removal as he died from Bright's disease in 1910.

Even though Reeves has never gotten credit for the many of his tactics, Hollywood has long taken ideas from his life to write plots for Western heroes. Not only was the character, the Lone Ranger, based around the exploits and stories of Reeves, but his sidekick, Tonto, was based on Reeves's partner, Grant Johnson (an African-American Indian) and shows a great deal of resemblance. Grant Johnson was not just any sidekick running behind a hero, but his stories are so compelling that he could have his own show. Even though there are no concrete facts to say that the Lone Ranger is in fact Bass Reeves, many historians suggest that the ideas of the show are not coincidental.

Despite his decades of service in the interests of law, Reeves lies in an unmarked grave and for years his legends were lost amongst history. Even more horrendous is the manner in which his stories and adventures were given to us. Reeves is not remembered as Wyatt Earp in a movie that shows his hero-like qualities (even though much of Tombstone was exaggerated). Nor is there a movie that makes Reeves a historical, poetic figure captivated in time like Billy the Kid, Jesse James, or Doc Holiday. In fact, lovers of Westerns are not even familiar with the man to whom a lot of stories were based upon. So instead of seeing Reeves when lawmen are mentioned, we see "The Duke," John Wayne.

What does Bass Reeves mean to us today? As a child, I remember playing "Cowboys and Indians" and mimicking many of the gestures that I saw watching television with my grandfather. I had the smooth, subtle moves of Matt Dillion as he approached a duel, the commanding and solemn look of John Wayne, and the "don't play with me" demeanor of Clint Eastwood. As children we patterned our experiences after what we viewed on television, so to us the white cowboys were always the heroes. What if we had known about Bass Reeves as children? Would that have sparked self-pride in our race? I remember seeing the Black Panther at the movies and leaving with such a feeling of pride and a newfound appreciation for being black. I wonder if that same pride and appreciation would have been felt as a child had my teacher taught Reeves or if there was a movie that highlighted his story.

Chapter

6

Britt Johnson (The Real Duke)

Britt Johnson was born a slave in eitherTennessee or Kentucky in 1840. His slave master was Moses Johnson and even though the words "slave master" never sits well in our thinking, Mr. Johnson was more compassionate and fair than many of the masters of his time. In fact it was his wish to set Britt free, but both agreed that it was too risky at that time. So instead Britt was appointed foreman of a ranch in Young County and was given his own horses and cattle. He was also given special permission to come and go as he pleased (a high honor to have as a slave).

As the legend goes, it was on October 13th 1864 that Britt and some other ranchers went to Weatherford for winter supplies when Little Buffalo and 700 Comanche braves raided Elm Creek. They stole most of the horses and cattle from the ranch and the other animals were killed. The braves surrounded the home of Mrs. Elizabeth Fitzpatrick. Inside the house with her were her children, Joseph and Susan, her two grandchildren, Charlotte and Millie Jan, and Britt's wife, Mary and their three children. According to most accounts, Susan ran out of the house with a gun. She was quickly overtaken, stripped, raped, and mutilated in the yard by the braves. Britt's oldest son was killed trying to protect the others who were eventually kidnapped.

Upon their return, many of the men were disheartened by the events that occurred. Many sought revenge but it was too risky to go after 700 Comanche braves. So they spent the winter rebuilding homes and sewing crops. During this time, Britt's master made him a free man and gave him half of his gold, so Britt could find his family. Britt was able to convince Chief Milky Way, also known as Asa- Havie to trade for Mrs. Fitzpatrick. After her freedom was granted, Britt returned Mrs. Fitzpatrick to her home and for his bravery, she gave him part of her wealth to help him rescue others.

Financed by Mrs. Fitzpatrick and Allen Johnson, Britt made three more trips into the Indian Territory rescuing surviving captives from the Elm Creek Raid. It was on his fourth trip that Britt rescued his family and the last of the captives, everyone except Millie Jane. It is believed that Millie Jane was adopted by Chief Au-Soat-Sai-Mah and her name changed to Sain-Toh-Oodie. A lie was invented to conceal her identity from whites looking for her. She married a brave named Goombi and they had nine children.

After the Civil War, Britt (already a free man) was granted official freedom along with his family. He moved to Parker County and set up a very successful freight business. He was the first black to receive government contracts for hauling freight with help from the government policy that favored business contracts for black freedmen. For six years Britt's company was the busiest freight business in the West; however, on January 24, 1871, Britt's fate would meet a devastating outcome. Britt was leading a wagon train through Young County delivering supplies from Weatherford to Fort Griffin when a group of Kiowa Indians attacked them. Johnson and two other men tried to defend the train but were outnumbered and lacked defensive shelter. By many accounts, it is stated that responders counted 173 rifle and pistol shells around the area Johnson's body was found. It is also documented that Johnson and his two companions had been scalped by the Kiowa and their mutilated bodies were placed in a grave next to the wagon road.

Britt Johnson is a forgotten figure on the Western Frontier.

However, many of his accomplishments were not forgotten as one of the major victories of his life was portrayed by John Wayne in the movie, *Searchers*. Fans of John Wayne, "The Duke," will recall how the movie was called the greatest American Western by the American Film Institute in 2008 and seen as the Duke's greatest performance. In 1989 the film was deemed "culturally and historically significant" by the United States Library of Congress and even preserved in the National Film Registry.

My complaint is not about the success of *Searchers*, but how a movie taken from the pages of history does not propel the actual person to stardom. *The Lone Ranger* was a success, but Bass Reeves has gained little national exposure; now we see the success of the movie, *Searchers*, yet many of you have never heard of Britt Johnson. This is a mind-blowing mystery that exposes the obvious correlation between the movie and the legend. The mere fact that Britt Johnson's wife, Mary, and their children were kidnapped by the Comanche tribe, eventually rescued by Johnson, and his granddaughter Millie Jane (who was never found but later discovered to have lived out her life as the adopted daughter of Chief Asa-Havie) is too coincidental to be ignored.

Some historians lead you to believe that the movie, *Searchers,* is actually based on Cynthia Ann Parker, not Millie Jane. They also fail to admit that the actual Elm Creek Raid searcher is Britt Johnson. I am always afraid of historians that leave out important details. This kind of foolery has led us to believe that Cesare Borgia's face is actually what Jesus would have looked like, but I digress. The problem lies in the fact that this oversight or cover-up has been attempted to be corrected by many historians such as Gregory Lalire, Scott Zesch, and Caroline Clemmons. However, even though the topic and current truths are available, Hollywood has yet to act on this matter in a way that brings this truth to national attention. But regardless of truth, history will recognize Cynthia Ann Parker and John Wayne's characters more than Millie Jane and Britt Johnson.

Now let's be fair to history as well: it is obvious that in the 1950s, homage could not be paid to an African American man for his story. The fact that black face and segregation was accepted in the nation leads us to speculate it was in the best interest of the creators of *Searchers* to omit these truths from history. However, I suggest that allowing this cover-up to continue robs many African Americans and/or minorities a clear place of existence in the establishment of both the West and national movie recognition. Yes, *Django Unchained* was a commercial success, but in all its glory, *Django,* based on the history of other similar films, will never have the opportunity to be preserved by the National Film Registry.

Chapter

7

Nat Love (Deadwood Dick)

Nat Love was born in June of 1854 to enslaved parents: Sampson Love, who was a foreman and his mother, (name unknown) who worked in the kitchen on Robert Love's plantation in Davidson County, Tennessee. Love would spend his childhood working the plantation like other children. After President Abraham Lincoln's *Emancipation*, Love's parents decided to stay on the plantation as sharecroppers instead of migrating north like other slaves on the plantation. According to historians, Love wanted more than life on the plantation and he dreamed of living life away from the limited opportunities blacks had in Tennessee. In February of 1869, Love left plantation life and headed west with $50 in his pocket.

Love traveled to Dodge City, Kansas and quickly found work as a cowboy on the Duval Ranch located in Texas. His hiring involved his boss agreeing that Love could join them if he could break a horse named Good Eye. But Good Eye was anything but good. In fact Good Eye was so wild that he broke bones of the workers on the ranch. Love would later recant that Good Eye was the toughest ride he'd ever had, but Love broke the horse and got the job earning thirty dollars a month. At 16 years old, Love quickly embraced the life of a cowboy. He showed excellent skills as a rancher and his shooting skills made him known as one of the fastest, most accurate shooters in the west. Love quickly moved up the ranks on the Duval Ranch where he became a buyer and their chief brand reader. His position sent him on numerous trips to Mexico where he learned to speak fluent Spanish.

After working faithfully for the Duval Ranch, Love moved to Arizona in 1872 and started working for the Gallinger Ranch. During these years Love traveled extensively throughout the west and many times in dangerous situations as he herded cattle to market. It was during this time that Love was referred to as Red River Dick and by many accounts entertained the company of famous men of the West such as Pat Garrett and Billy the Kid. In 1876, he attended an Independence Day event held in Deadwood, South Dakota. One of the events featured was a cowboy contest with a $200 cash prize to the winner. The contest featured roping, shooting, and saddling. Each event was won by Love, and he was given the nickname of "Deadwood Dick."

Love wrote in his journal that in October 1877, he was captured by a band of Pima Indians while he rounded up stray cattle in Arizona. He claimed to have received approximately 14 bullet wounds throughout his life as a cowboy. He wrote that his life was spared because of the respect the Indians had for his heritage. Many historians of the west fail to include the mixed blood between Native Americans and African Americans. The band of Indians nursed him back to health, hoping to adopt Love into their tribe. According to Love, he stole a pony and escaped into western Texas. Love would continue to work as a cowboy for another fifteen years before deciding to settle down and get married in 1889. He would take a job in Denver, Colorado as a Pullman porter traveling throughout the west. Nat Love died in 1921. Love's story, _The Life and Adventures of Nat Love_, was published in 1907 and has been reprinted several times since the 1960s. What is interesting about the story told by Love is that he condemns slavery but never recalls a time of any prejudices he faced in the West. He loved the Western Frontier so much that he looked on it with pride and honor for having become a great American story. He portrayed his story of the West as his freedom to transform from just a man to a hero.

I, along with many others would be, I'm sure, am bewildered by the lack of respect given to Nat Love. The fact that no movie has been created to portray his place in history is one thing, but I cannot begin to justify that the only movie that even talks about him is a Western comedy, *The Cherokee Kid*. This movie did not pay proper homage to the narrative of Nat, but instead established him as a bank robber facing public hanging before being saved by the main character. This attempt by Hollywood to display an African American actor in the role of a Western hero is inarguably the poorest attempt to cement our place as essential to the history of the Western Frontier.

The production itself was impressive and enjoyable. However, the usage of a historical figure in a way that offends their legacy is demeaning and harsh. What is sad is Hollywood would have profited more by using a fictional character than to use a historical hero in an inaccurate manner. The true image of Nat could have never been displayed in a more defamatory than in *The Cherokee Kid*. He was neither a bank robber nor criminal. He did not lead a band of miscreants nor solicit the services of hypocritical nuns in order to rob bands and kill the innocent. Why must we take such a hard defense in such a matter you may ask? My answer to such a question would simply be that most Americans are either ignorant to history or do not take time to care about the facts, so an inaccurate version of history becomes history to most.

Regardless of its humorous intent or the fact that the creators of the movie can and will say that this was not based on historical truths, the usage of the name Nat Love, when those of my generation hear it, does not point us in the direction of the real Nat Love, but the fictional portrayal outlined in the movie. So instead of seeing a true hero, we see a comical historical figure known for bank robberies with nuns and a man shot down in a semi-heroic manner, semi-heroic meaning a bank robber killed for avenging the hero's mother's death. When there are opportunities to introduce historian heroes to generations that are not aware of their history, one must take a serious look into presenting them in the correct, respectable manner.

Nat Love should represent for us the spirit of the west. The story of those escaping the harsh and regrettable years of slavery, looking to the west as a place of redemption. To many former slaves, the west served as an exclamation point to the independence so long deserved. It was the beginning of a new life where the land was rich and with hard work, men could actually be men with the fears of chains, whips, masters, and broken families diminished. Love showed us a man dedicated to his craft, and his reward should be a respect for his legacy and others who impacted the west with their boldness.

Chapter

8

Willie Bill Pickett
(The Dusky Demon)

One of the most famous African Americans of the West is none other than Willie "Bill" Pickett, especially to those who enjoy the sport of rodeo. Bill Pickett was born around December 5, 1870 in Williamson County near the Travis County line, Texas. He was one of thirteen children born to Thomas Jefferson Pickett and his wife, Mary Virginia Elizabeth Gilbert Pickett, and was the descendent of the American Indians and slaves. Bill learned to ride and rope horses at an early age. Many stories suggest that Bill began breaking horses at a young age as well. After completing the fifth grade, he went to work on a ranch.

Bill learned to "bulldog" a steer (male bull not used for reproducing) by grabbing it by the horns, twisting its neck, biting its nose or upper life, and making it fall on its side. The biting technique, he learned by observing herder dogs and how they controlled the steers. Soon he and his four brothers established their own horse breaking business in Taylor, Texas, called "Pickett Brothers Bronco Busters and Rough

Riders." During this time Bill became known by the simple tricks he performed in town on the weekends. News of this black man who could do horse tricks spread fast and soon Bill was asked to enter the world of entertainment.

In 1890 Bill performed in a Mexican bullfighting ring after one of the Miller brothers made a bet with the locals that Bill could ride a Mexican fighting bull for five minutes. Mexican fighting bulls, at the time, were some of the wildest animals and many saw this as suicide just to gain 5,000 pesos ($225 in 1890). Bill stayed on the bull for seven minutes and won the bet. However, Bill broke three ribs and was severely gashed by the animal. The Mexican crowd was furious and saw Bill's act as disrespect for their Mexican bullfighting tradition. The angry crowd threw bottles and trash at Bill and the other cowboys until police showed up.

In 1900 Bill became a showman, sponsored by Lee Moore, a Texas rodeo entrepreneur. Between 1905 and 1907, he signed with the Miller Brothers' 101 Ranch Wild West Show which featured stars like Will Rogers, Tom Mix, and Buffalo Bill Cody, becoming one of the star performers handling both wild and domestic animals. During this time, Bill earned the nickname "Dusky Demon." In the off seasons, Bill worked as a cowboy and competed against white contestants in rodeos around the West even though racial tensions in the United States were not favorable to African Americans. Bill would have to pose as Indian instead of African American to enter these shows. Bill won crowds over with his excitement in rodeo. Bill opened the door to respect for people of color in the West through his performances, and soon white audiences showed up to see him more than any other performer.

Bill married Maggie Turner, a former slave and the daughter of a white plantation owner. The couple had nine children. Bill performed until 1916 and is credited with inventing the technique of bulldogging, the skill of grabbing cattle by the horns and wrestling them to the ground. Bill was also an actor as he appeared in the silent films, *Crimson Skull* in 1921 and *The Bull Dogger* in 1922. This was the first movie that showed an African American man playing himself and telling his own Western story. African Americans felt pride because so many had never seen African American cowboys. On April 2, 1932, Bill died of injuries resulting from being kicked in the head by a horse he was breaking at the 101 Ranch. Bill's career in the sport of rodeo spanned over four decades and took him millions of miles in travel to entertain.

In 1971 Bill Pickett was inducted into the Rodeo Hall of Fame of the National Cowboy and Western Heritage Museum. In 1989 he was inducted into the Pro Rodeo Hall of Fame. Bill is the most celebrated African American person of the West. In 1993 the United States Postal Service created a commemorative sheet of stamps of Bill; however, the image had to be changed due to the face on the stamp being Bill's brother and fellow cowboy star, Ben Pickett. There are statues of Bill in Taylor, Texas, and the street leading to the rodeo arena is renamed to honor Bill Pickett.

The legend of Bill Pickett is one of courage in spite of racism. The same racism that plagued the greatness of many African American athletes is the same narrative that Pickett's life followed. He not only was great in his sport, but his contributions to the sport were key to its foundations. Many youth would frown on rodeo. Some will say the sport is for the white race only. However, Bill Pickett and his brothers brought skills to rodeo that will long be impactful to the sport. Like so many African Americans in the West, Bill came from modest beginnings and in spite of every obstacle, he strived to be the best he could be.

Although Bill Pickett's name has some value, it wasn't until after his death that his name gained momentum. It would be his great-grandson, Frank S. Phillips, Jr. that helped historians learn so much about Bill Pickett. Frank shared the stories his grandmother, Bessie Pickett Phillips (Bill's second oldest daughter), told him of his grandfather. These stories suggested that it was Bill and cowboys like him that made the way of the cowboy still a part of the Western culture. Amazingly these stories are not shown as a part of our culture in movies and television. There are only narratives of being black dominated by Thug Life or gangster fabulous living. For half a century, Hollywood has shown black living through the eyes of hood living or with racial overtones of living in the South. What it means to be black and raised in the ways of cowboys is rarely shown to the masses. But couldn't Bill Pickett be the hero of blacks outside of the West?

Chapter

9

Lesser Known Names

Mary Fields (Stagecoach Mary):

Mary Fields was born into slavery in Hickman County, Tennessee in 1832. Little is known about her early life, but she was freed when slavery was outlawed in 1865. In the late 1870s, she went to work as a housekeeper in the home of Judge Edmund Dunne. Mary was close to the family and they admired her strength and the compassion she showed to their five children. When Dunne's wife, Josephine, died in 1883, Mary took the five children to their aunt, Mother Mary Amadeus, who served as the Mother Superior of the Ursuline Convent in Toledo, Ohio.

Mary became the housekeeper at the convent and her friendship with Mother Mary Amadeus blossomed. Some accounts suggest that Mother Amadeus was a member of the family that owned Mary when she was a child, and the guilt of that encounter suggests that Mary was given special favor from Mother Amadeus. Even without special favor, Mary could handle her own. She was about 6 feet tall and weighed about

200 pounds. According to historian, Dee Garceau-Hagen, it is said that Mary's wrath is one that set the standard for how whites respected her. Mary's boldness proved vital as she tussled with the nuns over her wages. This behavior was shocking as white women expected African Americans to be submissive and "well behaved."

In 1885 Mother Amadeus was transferred to Montana, and shortly after, Mary moved with her. In many accounts, Mother Amadeus was near death with pneumonia and she needed Mary to take care of her. Mary traveled to Montana with the five children and nursed Mother Amadeus back to health. As the story goes, Mary's quick temper and no nonsense attitude got her kicked out of the convent when she pulled out a gun during an argument with the janitor at the convent. For the next ten years, Mary did jobs that were shocking for a woman of color during the 19th century standards of living. She started a few businesses and became known for indulging in hard liquor and gunfights. Mary was known as a woman that men feared and in all her gunfights, she was never shot.

In 1895 Mary (in her early sixties) was contracted from the United States Postal Service to become a Star Route Carrier. A Star Route Carrier, according to the position in 1895, was an independent contractor who used a stagecoach to deliver the mail in the harsh weather of Northern Montana. Delivering mail in 1895 cannot be compared to delivering mail today. Mail carriers were often robbed by mail thieves and/or killed. Mary used a stagecoach donated by Mother Amadeus. She was only the second woman in the United States to serve in this role and the first African American woman. Mary was known to travel with her trusted rifle and revolver and was known throughout the West as "Stagecoach Mary" or "Black Mary." Known for her heavy drinking and the fact that she wore men's clothing, Mary's sexuality was often questioned.

For eight years, Mary protected and delivered mail, money, and valuables over rough terrain. Oftentimes she was met with harsh weather, would- be thieves, and attacks from the Sioux tribes, but Mary prevailed. One story suggests that when she was faced with snow too deep for her horses to travel successfully, Mary strapped the mail bags over her shoulder and walked miles to the post office. On another mission, Mary's wagon was attacked by wolves which caused the scared horses to overturn her wagon. It is said Mary kept the wolves away throughout the night with her revolver. The story ends with Mary carrying all of the packets to the convent on her back.

In 1901 Mary retired from the mail service and opened a laundry in Cascade, Montana. She was well-known and loved in her community. Hollywood actor Gary Cooper met Mary as a youngster and deeply admired her. In 1912 Mary's laundry and home caught fire and burned to the ground. The people of Cascade came together and built her a new home. In 1914 Mary died of liver failure at the age of 82 years old.

Stagecoach Mary is starting to gain some traction in modern culture. An account of her life is currently being released to give today's audience a look into her legend. We can only hope that these accounts tell her story and not a fictitious account in order to gain a cult following like so many of the Hollywood produced movies. Today's generation has the power of the internet which makes research simply a click of the button and not a mission to through the library. With that being said, it is easy for our generation to mistake fiction for fact and to build an understanding on untruths. Mary serves as a symbolic symbol of the power for African American women. She, like so many others, had to be strong in a world dominated by men. Sojourner Truth, Harriet Tubman, Rosa Parks, Dr. Betty Shabazz, and Angela Davis are just a few who carried that strength as well. Mary had two things working against her: her race and her gender.

Mary was able to establish herself in the West although it was only a place that promoted women as helpless or submissive to the men that gained notoriety. Many historians in their writings have misrepresented women and led to the ignorant displace of endearment often seen in Hollywood productions. According to an article written in 2015 in Zocalo Public Square, women were afforded opportunities in the West that were not available to them in the East, such as the right to vote and more liberal divorce laws. Mary was so respected that the entire town of Cascade appreciated her service to the nation, and this appreciation lifted her higher than any black person in the West besides Bill Pickett. Mary is a symbol of courage, dedication, and inspiration to the character that has been a staple in the papers of the African American woman.

Ned Huddleston (Isom Dart) The Cattle Rustler:

Ned Huddleston is known to the Western Frontier as Isom Dart. He was born into slavery in 1849 in Arkansas. During the years of the Civil War, Ned served as a cook for a group of Confederate officers. He also nursed wounded soldiers, but his main job was stealing goods and food for the Confederate Army. This skill of stealing would later serve Ned as his one number job skill in the West.

Ned decided that Texas was the place to start a new life. In route to Texas, he stopped to work as a cook at the Carmicle railroad in the Wyoming Territory near Rock Springs, Wyoming. A coal mining and railroad town known for its diversity and outlaws, yet still reflective of the racism of the time, Ned was given the nickname "Nigger Ned." Like many African Americans of the time, racism as ugly as it was, was used as motivation to do more with one's life. Ned's determination to perfect the skill of shooting soon earned him the more respectable nickname, "Quick Shot," after firing his six shooter leaving five chickens headless in under three seconds.

Ned traveled to Texas then Mexico. According to his legend, this was the time in which Ned started his criminal activity, after deciding that being a rodeo clown was not a productive career. He would go into Mexico, steal horses and then go back to Texas to sell the horses. Ned quickly gained the notoriety of being an outlaw, and he took his roguish behavior to Northern Colorado where he added gambling to his wild lifestyle.

In 1875 he also joined the Tip-Gault Gang in Southeastern Wyoming. One evening the Gault Gang was burying a member who was killed by a kicking horse. As the group closed their eyes to offer up a moment of silence for their fallen friend, they were ambushed by a group of cowboys seeking revenge for an earlier incident. Every member of the gang was killed except for Ned, who according to legend, jumped into the grave and played dead. After several hours, Ned eventually crawled out of the grave and stole a horse from a nearby ranch. The rancher spotted him and shot Ned in the leg as he escaped. He was able to make it several miles before the loss of blood caused him to fall off of the horse and pass out. He was found and nursed back to health by his childhood friend, William "Billy Buck" Tittsworth.

In 1890 he brought a ranch near Brown's Hole and that's when he changed his name to Isom Dart. Trying to live a better life, Dart removed himself from the horse rustling life and for a period of time, enjoyed the simple life of ranching. By 1899 the Brown's Park territory war was intense with the Two-Bar Ranch Cattle Company and the Snake River Stock Growers Association attempting to push out small ranchers. Dart joined Ann Bassett, known to the area as "Queen Ann," who ran the Bassett Ranch. Queen Ann had an ongoing battle with Two-Bar Ranch's owner, Ora Haley, who accused Ann of cattle rustling. Stories vary on the motive of hiring notorious range detective, Tom Horn. Some accounts suggest that Haley hired Horn because he was tired of Ann and Dart stealing his cattle; other accounts suggest that Horn was hired to run small ranches out of the territory.

Isom Dart received a notice ordering him to leave the Brown's area along with other smaller ranchers. The fear of Tom Horn was great, and many of the ranchers packed up and left the area. Dart repudiated to leave his home in Routt County, Colorado. This decision would prove grave. On the morning of October 3, 1900, Dart was shot and killed by Tom Horn at 51 years old as he walked out of his cabin door, but some accounts suggest it was a man named James Hicks who shot and killed Dart because of the 30-30 shell casings found nearby. Later suggestions have added to the intensity of the story, suggesting that Tom Horn was in fact James Hicks. No one was ever charged in the killing of Dart. Ironically, Tom Horn was later hanged for the alleged murder of teenage sheepherder, Willie Nickell.

Isom Dart's story is like a tragic Shakespearean play. Sadly, the short period of his life as a gambler and rustler overshadow the many years of his life that made him a kind man. Dart is reputed to have never shot a man, even though he has threatened to do so a few times. According to some stories, Dart was elected to the office of Constable in Sweetwater County, Wyoming in 1884. Dart's assassination was seen as a cowardly act and it upset many of those in the Wyoming Territory. He was not viewed as attempting to steal cattle, but as a man defending his right against a larger corporation.

Crawford "Cherokee Bill" Goldsby "The Outlaw":

Crawford "Cherokee Bill" Goldsby is one of the most famous outlaws of the west to be so unknown by most Americans. He was just as ruthless as known outlaws such as Jesse James or Billy the Kid. Crawford was born in Fort Concho, Texas on February 8, 1876. He is the son of a Cherokee Indian mother, Ellen, and an African-American "Buffalo Soldier" from the 10th Cavalry, Sergeant St. George, a freedman mixed with African, Indian, and white ancestry. By the time he was seven years old, his parents had separated and his mother moved him to the Indian Territory near Fort Gibson. His dad was eventually driven out of Texas by the Ku Klux Klan. According to various accounts, Crawford was sent to several schools for a good education, but he could barely read and write.

Crawford left school at 12 years old. It was at this age that it is said Crawford killed his first man. As the story goes, Crawford confronted his brother-in-law who had told him to feed some hogs. After a huge confrontation ensued over the chores, Crawford shot and killed his brother-in-law. He managed to escape punishment due to his age; however, this murder would not be the last one by his hand. A year later, his mother remarried to a man that did not like him. Crawford and his stepfather had heated arguments three to four times a week.

It was around this time that Crawford started hanging out with a bad crowd of individuals who introduced him to drinking liquor and a rebellious lifestyle. By the time he was 17 years old, Crawford was working on a ranch. He was well-liked by those who worked with him and showed signs of having a great career in ranching.

At 18 years old, Crawford shot Jake Lewis for beating up his younger brother. Even though Lewis would later recover from his wounds, Crawford thought he killed him, fled Fort Gibson and traveled to live among the Creek and Seminole Indian Nations. It was during this time that he met outlaws—Jim and Bill Cook. The authorities tracked Crawford and an ensuing shoot-out between Crawford and the authorities left lawman, Sequoyah Houston, dead. Crawford was officially an outlaw now. He soon found refuge in his sister, Maud's home. However, Crawford grew furious at Maud's abusive husband,

George Brown, for beating on her. One night George, a vicious drunk, began to beat Maud with a whip for not responding quickly enough to his orders. So like his other brother-in-law, Crawford shot and killed him.

Crawford knew that there was no chance of going back to a normal life. He was a wanted man with little resources, family, and friends. He decided to rejoin the Cook brothers and change his name to "Cherokee Bill" and began a crime spree that put many on edge. Crawford quickly became one of the most wanted and feared men in the Indian Territory. There was a $1,300 reward (almost $50,000 today) dead or alive for him. On August 2, 1894, the gang was surrounded by the authorities at the home of a friend in Oklahoma. After a gunfight ensued, one of the lawmen was severely wounded. Two of the gang members, Lon Gordon and Henry Munson were killed and another member was captured. The rest of the gang fled the scene with no injuries.

The gang's most profound crime was the hold-up of the depot of the Missouri Pacific Railroad. After robbing the station, the gang rode two hours and robbed the railway agent in the next town. Ten days later, they caused the wreck of the Kansas City and Pacific Express before robbing it. Between August and October, Crawford and the Cooks robbed and mercilessly killed anyone that got in their way. It was also during this time that Crawford's hair started to fall out due to a disease inherited by this grandfather. According to his legend, the moment he shaved off his hair, he became more brutal. Many men were killed by Crawford, most of them workers on the railway or postal service carriers, some bank tellers, and some lawmen. While robbing the Shufeldt and Son General Store, an innocent passerby named Ernest Melton heard the commotion and decided to investigate the scene. He stuck his head in the door and was killed when Crawford shot him in the head at close-range with a rifle.

Crawford's evasion of the authorities ran out on January 30, 1895. With the assistance of acquaintances wanting to cash in on the reward, Crawford was captured and delivered to Fort Smith, Arkansas to await trial for the murder of Ernest Melton in the general store robbing. Crawford was found guilty by Judge Parker and sentenced to be hanged. Crawford had one more trick up his sleeve. On July 26, 1895, a friend smuggled Crawford a pistol into his cell. The shootout resulted in one of the guards being killed and a standoff ensued. The guards were unable to disarm Crawford. However, also in jail was a man even more notorious and feared than Crawford, an outlaw named Henry Starr. The guards got Starr to persuade Crawford into surrendering. Starr agreed only if a deal was made to not kill Crawford once disarmed. When agreed, Starr walked into Crawford's cell and after a short conversation, he walked out of the cell with Crawford's pistol and handed it to the guards. This act of bravery on Starr's part would eventually lead to his freedom and his charges dismissed by President Theodore Roosevelt in 1901.

After several appeals were made to get Crawford a new trial, he was hanged on March 17, 1896 in front of hundreds of spectators. It is reported that when asked if he had any final words, he said: "I came here to die, not to make a speech." Crawford "Cherokee Bill" Goldsby was only 20 years old at the time of his death. His mother took his remains back to the Fort Gibson area where he is buried at the Cherokee National Cemetery. It is reported that Crawford killed eight men in his life, and one of the guards later stated that Crawford said: "This is as good a day to die as any" as he stepped into the courtyard and saw the gallows. This phrase is historically associated with certain Native American cultures.

According to legends on the Indian Territory, Crawford "Cherokee Bill" Goldsby's legend is as important to history as that of Billy the Kid or Jesse James. Even though we do not glorify his actions, we cannot ignore the importance of outlaws on the Western Frontier. Men like Billy the Kid and Jesse James have become cemented in the legends that make up the Western Frontier. In fact Billy the Kid and Jesse James have become more famous than many of the lawmen that served the West heroically. Many will ask why Crawford is even mentioned in this literary work or why his story must be told. To avoid Crawford's story is like getting rid of the history attributed to any bad guy in history. Adolf Hitler, Jim Jones, and even Charles Manson have literary works and even films to show their ascent to insanity. Should Crawford "Cherokee Bill" Goldsby's story not be mentioned to give us some insight into what made a good rancher decide to be an outlaw? Actors R. G. Armstrong, L.Q. Jones, and Albert Salmi built their careers by playing villains in Westerns, which show us the need for bad guys.

Chapter

10

The Power of Knowledge

The greatest crime committed is the withholding of knowledge. In fact the Bible states that a people will perish due to the lack of knowledge. The fact that black cowboys, ranchers, or even a black woman stagecoach driver was never taught in schools continues the downward slope of a loss of identity. I remember laughing at Charley Pride for singing country music as a child. I thought a black man singing country music was a sell-out to his race. Seeing him dressed like a Western Crooner with white people in the audience was unbelievable to me. I was used to rappers, hip hop, R&B, and gospel singers; but a black man singing country was an anomaly. I did not realize that he was continuing a legacy of blacks that sang songs on the Great Frontier, songs that started as hymns but with the stroke of guitar turned into the foundation of what is now country music.

It was not my generation only that missed the value in Charley Pride, but maybe others before me. During ages of racial oppression and the creation of new identities during the Civil Rights Movement, I can only imagine Charley Pride being seen as a sell-out instead of a hero, even though he had 39 No. 1 singles and was second only to Elvis Presley in albums sold for RCA records. Charley fought through racial oppression more than most singers during his time. He faced backlash from whites and blacks for sounding white but being black. Most listeners and radio programmers did not realize he was black when he first hit the radio in the 1960s.

Few African Americans have heard of DeFord Bailey, a world-class harmonica player, who was the first country singer or musician to be introduced on the Grand Ole Opry on December 10, 1927. Amazingly the true acceptance of an African American country singer to African Americans was either Darius Rucker, Cowboy Troy or Lil Nas X. Lil Nas X set new standards with this record-selling song "Old Town Road." For the first time since the Gap Band, it was cool for a black artist to wear cowboys' attire on stage in front of a black audience. What is more of an awakening is that even though Lil Nas X introduced many in this generation to black culture outside of the norm, he actually sparked curiosity into a world that never forgot its deep roots in American history. Such groups as the Compton Cowboys are examples that understanding history is key to a brighter future. Many lives have been saved because of the Compton Cowboys battling the streets, drugs, and gangs through horses and history.

In 1977 Lu Vason, an African American from California, realized black cowboys were not getting enough attention at the Cheyenne Frontier Days, a massive rodeo and festival held in Wyoming. He decided to create the Bill Pickett Invitational Rodeo in 1984. He made sure that the event would ensure black rodeo athletes. The success of the rodeo attracted black rodeo athletes from all over the states and was held as one of the biggest events for years. When Vason died in 2015, his widow assumed the position of promoter and CEO. Vason contributed to the sport largely and opened the door for black rodeo athletes that previously faced backlash regardless of their ancestors' contributions.

Even though times have changed, many black rodeo athletes still feel the wounds of racism. Unlike the National Football League (NFL), National Basketball Association (NBA), or Major League Baseball (MLB), rodeos are not embraced by African Americans as a majority in the United States. This means that in many areas, segregation is still prevalent in the sport. Jackie Robinson is celebrated for his heroic entrance into Major League Baseball, but who was the hero that integrated rodeos? Michael Jordan is considered the greatest NBA player to step on the court, but who is the greatest black rodeo athlete? Jim Brown was considered the most amazing black running back in the 60s in the NFL, but who was the showstopper when it came to the rodeo? Many will say this was a result of television programming, some will say it is demographics because rodeos and black cowboys are mainly of western importance, and some will argue that other sports make millionaires. However, I suggest that the lack of knowledge about __ (what?)__ is why Charley Pride is not a black superstar and why rodeos are not big sports within black culture.

I also suggest that a lack of knowledge about this topic is why black history starts at slavery, skips over 100 important years of knowledge, and then picks back up with the Civil Rights Movement. This keeps Black History content limited to Harriet Tubman, Frederick Douglas, Martin Luther King Jr., Rosa Parks, and Emmett Till. This limited information is why African Americans struggle with identity. Only two identities are left to be considered---being labeled as a "slave" or as a "nigger" based on narratives of common history. What have the narratives and Hollywood showed us about African American history? Harriet Tubman was a conductor on the Underground Railroad, but the heroic work she did as a Union spy is hardly mentioned. Rosa Parks refused to give up her seat on the bus, but nothing of the continued work she did for almost 50 years is expanded upon. Martin Luther King Jr. had a dream, but it is never discussed how Dr. King's rebellion against the status quo made him feared by the Federal Bureau of Investigations (FBI). Essential portions of African American history have been left out of history books, characters have been white-washed, stories have been changed, and Hollywood guides our history teachers.

So what is the power of knowledge? Many philosophers credit Sir. Francis Bacon with the powerful proverb: "knowledge is power." This proverb suggests that the usefulness of knowledge creates power in our human endeavors. For example, the knowledge of understanding that an iron is hot gives mankind the power to protect oneself from a burn. If the knowledge of history proves to be powerful, then we can say that understanding the Holocaust is essential to recognizing the traits of Hilter's dictatorship so that future leaders are not able to repeat history. However, the knowledge of history is not only powerful in prevention, but positive in the evolution of a culture.

When fire was created, mankind developed a more civilized world of eating, fighting, and warmth in its initial stages. However, fire continued to evolve into building bridges through welding, melting steel, creating advanced weaponry, and warming homes. Now we can even fry, bake, boil, or grill our foods. Cannot the knowledge of African Americans on the Great Frontier empower an oppressed race of people too? Those who are left to believe that their only contributions to American came through free labor and the struggle for equality? What if the forgotten heroes or villains were taught as those of Warp Earp or Jesse James? Would this knowledge lead to the power of prevention or evolution? Could a black youth see the short, reckless life of Cherokee Bill and decide not to follow a similar path, or see the law was the tool that made Bass Reeves a legend? These overlooked parts of history must be included so that they may become powerful pieces of knowledge that shape our futures for the better.

Book Reviews

C.T. Kirk explores a significant account on the history of Blacks and their contributions to the West. The role of Blacks and their contributions westward expansion has been largely overlooked in American history. The uninterrupted history of Blacks in the United States began in 1619, when 20 Africans were landed in the English colony of Virginia. This theoretical work will help to identify a rich literature and explore methodology the role of Blacks and Indians migrants westward as examined statistically to the treatment of Blacks by government in the United States.

Dr. Samuel L. Hinton

Higher Education Practitioner, Author, Researcher and CEO of HBCU NEXTG

"How the West was White-washed," is an important contribution to the American historical canon recording the advancement of the nation's western frontier. C.T. Kirk demonstrates the importance of expansive historical research in shaping the narrative of America's cultural evolution as e pluribus unum. This volume helps to extend the field, fill in the gaps, and finally perpetuate a more accurate and inclusive story of America. Likewise "How the West..." helps to counter the way that dominant stories further the myths of white superiority, black inferiority, and racial inequality, fracturing the hoped-for unity of the nation. In a powerful story of triumph, Kirk is able to recapture the "hidden Wakandas of the West," that were havens for heroic figures that are rarely mentioned or portrayed in the Hollywood pantheon of cowboy "superheroes" of the past.

These are heroes that our young children, and not-so-young children, can now finally celebrate and emulate.

Dr. Lester Agyei McCorn, President of Clinton College

For one to understand the complexity of their existence, a proper telling of one's history is needed. History, as the old adage, is written by the winners, which means those who are the ostracized and the overlooked have little representation historically. Historian and Author C. T. Kirk seeks to shed light on the egregious underrepresented tellings of the African-American in the context of Western culture in his literary offering, "How The West Was Whitewashed"

Replete with accurate historical data and nuanced research, Kirk sheds light on Western Culture from the perspective of those often left out of its telling-Black and Brown people. Kirk asserts that the inaccurate telling and retelling of Western Culture's history has not only damaged the legacy of the West, but has caused those who should embrace its tradition to be unaware of its existence.

The American Cowboy is an iconic figure, one used to anchor American folklore in the minds and hearts of many. Its leaving out of its Black and Brown players has caused a telling of history that is at its best unbalanced and its worse biased and negligent. Kirk's in depth research and his poignant portrayal of the Black cowboy brings both solace and sobriety to the reader, as one realizes the beauty in the Black Cowboys existence and the sadness that many have tried to hide the fact that he exists.

Terrance Culp, CEO of Culp Is Speaking, Author, Motivational Speaker

Bibliography

Acosta, Teresa Paloma. "Black Cowboys." *Handbook of Texas Online.* Texas State Historical Assn., 12 June 2010. Web. 30 Mar. 2015.

Bays, Brad A. "African American Cowboys." *Encyclopedia of the Great Plains.* U of Nebraska Lincoln, 2011. Web. 30 Mar. 2015.

Bailey C. Hanes, *Bill Pickett, Bulldogger: The Biography of a Black Cowboy* (Norman: University of Oklahoma Press, 1977).

Brook, Tom. "When White Actors play other Races". BBC Publishing. October 6, 2015. Retrieved from http://www.bbc.com/culture/story/20151006-when-white-actors-play-other-races

Dianna Everett, "Pickett, William," *The Encyclopedia of Oklahoma History and Culture,* https://www.okhistory.org/publications/enc/entry.php?entry=PI003.

Elofson, W. M. *Cowboys, Gentlemen and Cattle Thieves: Ranching on the Western Frontier.* Montreal: McGill-Queen's University Press. 2000. Accessed February 13, 2019. ProQuest Ebook Central

Glasrud, Bruce A. and Michael N. Searles (eds.) *Black Cowboys in the American West: On the Range, on the Stage, behind the Badge.* Norman, OK: University of Oklahoma Press, 2016.

Hanes, Bailey C. 1977. *Bill Pickett, Bulldogger: The Biography of a Black Cowboy.* Vol. 1st ed. Norman: University of Oklahoma Press. https://search-ebscohost-com.lopes.idm.oclc.org/login.aspx?direct=true&db=nlebk&AN=14878&site=ehost-live&scope=site.

Hardaway, Roger D. "African American Communities on the Western Frontier." *Communities in the American West.* Ed. Stephen Tchudi. Reno: Nevada Humanities Committee and U of Nevada P, 1999.

Hardaway, Roger D. "African American Cowboys." *Texas Ranch House.* WGBH, PBS, n.d. Web. 30 Mar. 2015.

Hoglund, Don A. "African American or Black Cowboys in the Western Frontier". *Owlcation Journal*. February 18, 2019. Retrieved from https://owlcation.com/humanities/African-American-cowboys-in-History-and-ictionf

Hughey, Matthew. "The White Savior Film: Content, Critics, and Consumption". Temple University. pp. 1-286. October 1, 2014

Jerrold J. Mundis, "He Took the Bull by the Horns," *American Heritage* (December 1967). "Bill Pickett," Vertical File, Rodeo Historical Society Hall of Fame, National Cowboy and Western Heritage Museum, Oklahoma City, Oklahoma.

Jordan, Terry G. *North American Cattle Ranching Frontiers: Origins, Diffusion, and Differentiation*. Albuquerque: U of New Mexico P, 1993. Print.

Kocurek, Carly A. "THE WHITE SAVIOR FILM: Content, Critics, and Consumption Matthew W. Hughey." *American Studies* 54 (2): 137. 2015. https://search-ebscohost-com.lopes.idm.oclc.org/login.aspx?direct=true&db=edsjsr&AN=edsjsr.24589477&site=eds-live&scope=site.

Love, Nat. *The Life and Adventures of Nat Love, Better Known in the Cattle Country as "Deadwood Dick"*. Lincoln: University of Nebraska Press, 1995.

Manzoor, Sarfraz. "America's Forgotten Black Cowboys." *BBC News*. BBC, 22 Mar. 2013. Web. 30 Mar. 2015.

McClellan, Michael E. "JOHNSON, BRITTON," *Handbook of Texas Online* (http://tshaonline.org/handbook/online/articles/fjo07), accessed March 19, 2020.

Nodjimbadem, Katie. "The Lesser-Known History of African-American Cowboys". *Smithsonian.com*. February 13, 2017. Retrieved from https://www.smithsonianmag.com/history/lesser-known-history-african-american-cowboys-180962144/

Rawlings-Carroll, R. (2010, August 26) Isom Dart (1849-1900). Retrieved from https://www.blackpast.org/african-american-history/isom-dart-1849-1900/

Salmon, Caspar. "Should We be Surprised by John Wayne's Racist and Homophobic Views?" *The Guardian*. 20 February 2019.

Retrieved from https://www.theguardian.com/film/2019/feb/20/
john-wayne-racist-homophobic-views-1971-playboy-interview

Turner, Frederick J... "Social Forces in American History." *The American
Historical Review* 16 (2): 217. 1911.

Washington, Margaret. "African American History and the Frontier
Thesis." *Journal of the Early Republic 13*, no. 2 (1993): 230-41. doi:
10.2307/3124089.

Wills, Matthew "Whitewashing American History". *Jstor Daily*.
February 18, 2019. Retrieved from https://daily.jstor.org/
whitewashing-american-history/

Printed in the United States
By Bookmasters